POETIC MUSINGS

About the Author

Jagdish Chandra Sharma was born in Lahore (now in Pakistan, then called the Paris of India). He migrated to India in 1947 as a penniless refugee after the partition of India, he received his MA. degree in Political Science in 1953, M.A. in English in 1955 from the Punjab University, Chandigarh

He Served as a lecturer in Political Science at Guru Ram Rai College, Nahan (H.P.) (Now Government College) from 1956 to 1962; Head of the Political Science Department at D.A.V. College Ambala from 1963 to 1968; Head of the Post-Graduate Department of Political Science at Dayanad (Evening) College, Hissar from 1968 to 1972; Principal, Mewat Degree College, Nagina (now Govt. College) from 1972 to 1975; Assistant Chief Editor, Section, Encyclopaedia of Indian Literature, National Sahitya Academy from 1975 to 1979; Editor, the Lions International; Delhi Branch; Chief Consultant, Chandra Export Agencies, New Delhi.

He also contributed from time to time to Caravan, Delhi, Illustrated Weekly of India, Bombay; Organiser, Delhi.

His publications: Gandhi the humanist (1964); Nehru the humanist (1965); The Political Philosophy of Jawahar Lal Nehru (1966). Indian Prime Ministership, (2002).

He also contributed short stories and poems in Urdu in Pasvan an Urdu Weekly published from Chandigarh.

POETIC MUSINGS

Dr. Jagdish Chandra Sharma

CONCEPT PUBLISHING COMPANY,
NEW DELHI-110059

Dedicated
to
Mrs. K. Chandra — Wife

Cataloging in Publication Data--DK
Courtesy: D.K. Agencies (P) Ltd. <docinfo@dkagencies.com>

Sharma, Jagdish Chandra, 1928-
Poetic musings / Jagdish Chandra Sharma.
p. cm.
Poems.
ISBN 81-8069-103-9
1. Indic poetry (English). I. Title.

DDC 821 21

ISBN: 81-8069-103-9
First Published 2004

Published and Printed by
Ashok Kumar Mittal
Concept Publishing Company
A/15-16, Commercial Block, Mohan Garden
New Delhi-110059 (INDIA)
Phones : 25351460, 25351794
Fax : 091-11-25357103
Email : publishing@conceptpub.com

Preface

Poetry is a passion. It has no particular time to erupt. Like a volcano it has its own time to erupt and after eruption it flows uncontrolled with the heat of images and thoughts. Our eyes act as lens of a camera. The mind serves as a reel and heart as the dark room where in darkness pictures develop. "*The heart wants what it wants... There is no logic to those things.*" Woody Allen.

Here scholarship is not wanted which takes lot of time and energy. I remember my previous work on Indian Primeministership which took me ten years to complete. I find poetry comparatively lighter, full of pleasure and joy. It has no particular time as it flows from the heart, any time, any place, under every kind of circumstances. Sometimes, at midnight one is aroused, heart dictates and one goes on writing. Even during inconvenient hours it comes like a cool breeze which gives one tranquillity, calm and cool. One feels elated, lost in oneself oblivious of one's surroundings. Things look differently, strongly with fascination under cover of super consciousness. The comfortable warmth can just be felt without any elucidation.

Abstract of review of the book, Indian Prime Ministership: A Comprehensive Study by Jagdish Chandra Sharma published in Marathi Daily on Saturday, the 11 May, 2002 in its editorial column.

In the beginning of the book the Author has given introduction in 20 pages that democracy existed in India in the remote past. There were republics in miniature. As a consequence India is surviving as a strong democracy.

Principal Sharma has written one chapter on the relationship between the Prime Minister and the President. He has also given in detail the debate between Dr. Rajendra Prasad and Dr. Ambedkar making some constitutional points very clear.

The benefits and drawbacks in the Parliamentary system of Government will be well understood by the readers of this book.

In conclusion, Principal J.C. Sharma has tried his best to study all aspects of the problem in details. It can be said that the author has given us comprehensive study of the vast powers of the Prime Minister.

Prof. Avinash Kolhe

Contents

The Boss

The Boss a cross
Warning of human failings
A headed cobra
Hissing all around.

Art of administration
A service of the nation
Make others believe
That you don't deceive.

Say one thing to one
And second to the other
An exercise in delusion
To both it gives satisfaction.

Diplomatic lies
Hows and whys
Never fight shy
Evade simple questions
Give vague replies.

Flap your wings
As protective angels do
Strike at the first moment
As the fiendish agents do.

Say yes to what he says
Say no to what he nayes
The modern monarch is he
And "King can do no wrong'.

Like a dutiful courtier
Keep your eyes on him
Smile when he smiles
Stand when he stands
Laud him as a Burke
A Churchill or Chanakya
Match his anger
With your hunger
To receive his ire
On your head
Ever be ready
His rebukes to wed.

With the air of sycophancy
You may inflate him
Beyond proportions
He may blow out
Into pieces.

Remember there is
Limit to all
things big or small
Must remain within the walls
If you have self respect
Think him no more
Than Don Juan,
Learn to defy him when you must.

City Life

How charming are
these sky-scrapers
the 'space-rapers'
looking up and up
in search of fairies
and ventures fresh.

The motley crowds milling around
like swarming bees
bound by invisible ties.

The fluorescent lights
bluish white
cripple the soul
and dazzle the eyes.

What a loneliness
midst this throng
that has no heart
no soul,
all stone.

The dragons of death
roam about
trampling life
yelling hell
spitting fire in pell-mell.

In the darkness
of night
in the lap of
mother earth
sleep and weep
the best creatures
created in God's own image,
an endless open-air hall
with no roof, with no wall.

The clouds of smoke
like a pall of dust
cover the whole city
showing up a
live grave-yard.

The butterflies
listen to phones
carry the germs
to Toms and Johns.

Delhi

My Delhi, My Dear Delhi
My beloved Delhi
Everyweek has a rally
How vast is her belly
Some in the name of God
And some in the name of Mammon
They impede the traffic
like a Demon.

Seven Times she died
Like Phoenix she has the power
to rise from the ashes
we are living in the
Eighth re-born Delhi

Sometimes it stops my water
and says don't waste it
this is the elixir of life
Sometimes it shuts my light
and advises, 'you have
worked hard, now take rest'

The seat of our rulers
Past, present and future
It is the heart of India

Mahatma told us to live
A poor man's life
We forcibly slept
Him in the lap of mother earth

We think we live
In the modern era
We must live like
Princes and not beggars

Lord Kirshna's Jamuna
Has become so old
Now it is neither silver
nor gold
It has some old memories
'Red Fort' or 'Qutab Minar'
We cannot forget big
markets of Karol Bagh, Chandni Chowk,
So full of life, not kill, they choke

You can buy all that you want
American, European or Asian.

At reasonable rates
don't bother about duplicate
so many places of interest
Trade Fair Unity in diversity reflects
Delhi haat a place
For meals of all states
At reasonable rates
You enjoy with your mate
With all love, no hate
Every Sunday you visit
any one to win over
the monotony of the week
She has served me like a wife
She has given me all the comforts of life.

Demonstrations

Wherefrom so many people came
With a faith in demonstration.
Cameras perched on roof tops
for pictures.

The size of the crowd
And size of the road
Had merged into one,
Lakhs of feet, lakhs of hands,
Lakhs of heads,
A python surging ahead,
Thousands of flags and slogans,
All of them suddenly lose their motio
Like ants they ran helter, skelter,
Disorder and confusion, no better,
Doors and Windows shut.
Sudden rise of the smoke,
Flames leaped up,
Shrieks and gun shots,
Stumbling and running
Trampling and injuring.

All was over in a few seconds,
All the procession melted
Into scattered shoes,
Broken chappals, flags,
Torn clothes, caps, broken sticks
And crumpled banners.
The police van packed
with miscreants and the wounded.
The so-called miscreants
taken to ten miles and released.
An announcement,
Many people were hurt
In the stampede,
The police opened fire
but all in the air
Bullets disappeared,
But where such a vast tragedy,
only one was killed
As God willed.
The corpse was taken to
the Police Station for
Post-mortem,
The situation was under control,
All peaceful and quiet.

Doctor

Doctor is next to God
Does it appear odd?
God we have not met
No one knows where he is set.

We can see doctor
We can tell him of our trouble,
He gives us hope
With our ailments he copes.
We go to him and weep
We run to him during his sleep.

He examines us,
Tests our blood or pus,
He may understand or guess.
He gives us medicine
Wipes our tears,
He may transplant heart,
Kidney and liver.
He may give us relief or cure,
He may amputate any

organ dangerously damaged
up to this he is all right.
When he starts thinking of money
He turns into a spoonful of honey
When he lusts for wealth
His every action is a stealth.
He makes us weep
He does not go deep
He is no longer next to god
He turns into a punishing rod.

An Evening on Shanghmugham Beach

On the sand are lying,
the young, the old and the kids
Feeling the warmth of the earth
from which they sprang
To which they will return

In the water are standing
Legs, the beautiful, the ugly,
the cigarette-like, the shrubby,
the shapely, the comely, of marble,
of black colour.

The waves are coming, touching
the feet of earth and rush back
to come again and again, the
mighty sea kisses the beloved beach
what does it teach?
Sea with passion of love is
violent, kisses the earth, she resists

The sun is rapidly going down.
The rays are falling like a
golden shower on her breasts,
The sea with his passion of love
shows the spirit of dove.

The sun is shaping
like pitcher, turning up and down
now like a dome of fire, now
a red crescent moon, engulfed by sea

From the Earth has come
The moon; one ruler of day is gone
the other one has come.
This drama goes on for ever.

Give me thorns, O God!

Beautiful are the roses
The velvet touch
The petals pink
The perfumes mix
They make you feel
they exist.

Lovely are the roses
Smiling are the poses
Coquettish roles
Festoon decked poles.

Life a campaign
A struggle, a fight
Aren't flowers plucked
Trampled and roughed?
Thorns resist
Pricks persist.

Thorns strike and warn
of all glory

Glories fade so soon
Glamours quickly swoon
Oh God! I ask for a boon
Give me thorns
And no roses
Enabling me to
Return the kicks
And pricks that
Life so generously
bestowed on me!

King of Coalitions—Vajpayee

Four decades saw India
under the rule of one party,
Lust for power and wealth
Eating into the Vitals
of Nation's health,
Left no place for satiety
Power corrupts, Absolute
Power absolutely,
Fovouratism, nepotism, corruption
ruled the roost to confusion
Storm of total revolution,
Declaration of emergency,
And mass arrests,
Family planning, forceful threats,
Then the engine of people's anger
Rolled down political monopoly
Small parties came forward
to become big
But they turned into pigs,
unstable and short-lived
At last came on the scene

Atal Bihari, Baal Brahmchari
He infused new
life into coalition
giving it strength and length
Ruling out demolition, keeping off diversity
Cementing unity in diversity.
He made his critics
realise that coalitions
Also worked well
To full terms
If patronised by wisdom
and endurance.
In fact he will
go down in history
As the king of coalitions.

Kovalam Beach

Sea is the sire with
Blue blood in his veins
Coming forward
Again and again
To kiss his beloved
earth
gets nothing else
but kicks
Is he under a curse?

If God is anywhere
Is n't He here?
With all his glory
Majesty and grandstory.

Here I see the living
sculptures from
the caves of Ajanta
Well-shaped hips
Breasts full round
Raw mangoes,

Juicy mangoes,
Oranges, red blood
And fresh,
Lemons pale and sallow
Flowers, white, pink,
Brown and yellow
A world in itself, fellow.

Tide always throws us up
And out, not down
Let's lift others up
No letting down
Or, the sea
At us
will frown.

Lahore – My Birth Place

When I was born
Lahore was a Paris then
All fashions like clouds
Rose and covered the whole
of India

Before nineteen forty seven
It was a heaven
For all those who lived there
Progressing on all sides, its
Population was ten lakhs against
Delhi's five,
For Social, Economic, Political
Religious gatherings a hub place
To run forward there was a race.

Pure milk was common,
Still a rarity in Hindustan
Sharif, Musharaf and Ibrahim
Played with me with enthusiasm,
one day one of their uncles

came from abroad
He was on ride of purety
He knew very little of India
He brainwashed my friends
And instructed them not to
Play with infidels,
Pakistan will be freed from all kafirs,
God will come down with
One of His seven heavens,
After clearance of all infidels.
It was, and still a riddle.
There was lot of bloodshed
Blue, black, yellow and red.
God has not come down
So far, nor His heaven
There were many picnic spots
Canal of Mian Mir, safe swimming
Lawrence Garden for jogging and running
River Ravi for boating.

Hira Mandi produced Nurjehan
Lata Mangeshkar of Pakistan

For Western India a focal
Point for trade,
Educational centre attracted
People like bees

Exhibitions, kite-flying
adorned Minto Park.
I still remember the
Life-pulsating lanes
Evergreen Model Town,
Historical places, Nurjehan tomb
And fort old
with glamorous festive rounds
Almost all Kafirs came to India
Even now patients with
No treatment facility there
come to Kafirs in India
And go back healthy with agility.

Modern Art

Modern Art
A confused mart
of ideas and images
Labour without wages
Spent in ages.

A mystic poem to go through
Meanings to woo
After the gaze
Scratching the head
Puzzled we stand
To condemn or praise.

Our own meanings
We put into it
Is n't it our own interpretation
That gives life
To the conglomeration?
Who invests the portrait
With a soul?
Are n't we also

the artists then
Real, part or whole?

Is n't it enough
to behold the colourful show,
The splendour of the rainbow
Violet, crimson, pink and yellow
Enough charm to bow
A reward in itself to know.

The suckers of the eyes
suck in the blood
of pleasure, a joy
without measure,
Delight is the end of life
Enough, Am I right?

Modern Guru

A God-fearing man
he is.
Why should he fear
A man,
He looks upon others
As God looks on us,
treats us like helpless
flies.
God keeps us, flies down
To keep sky clear
for his flights.
Guru is too big for the train
Aeroplane is his vehicle main
A modern God is he
Religion he presents as
a bundle of rituals
And no more.
He has learnt a lesson
God is also pleased
When devotees offer him oblations
He builds up air-conditioned

Ashram with marble floors,
He keeps open his doors
For those who can give
Rich donations.
He is the modern king
He looks upon offerings
A sign of loyalty and affection
A prayer in outright perfection.

My Country, My Bharat

The most ancient civilisation
The land of sears and saints
Punctuated by savage invasions
Nalanda and Taxila
Were burnt
But its spirit remained
unhurt
Two great rivers,
Hinduism and Buddhism surged
from this sea
And flooded the Eastern Asia
With sweet life-giving breeze
No jihad, no crusades, no tease.
Ahimsa Parmodharma.
Her goal of peace
Prithiviraj let off Ghasnavi
After the latter's every defeat,
A rare example of bravery
But Ghasnavi after his
First victory treated Prithivi savagely
A rare example of mental-slavery.
Nobel laureates in different fields

Raised the honour of my motherland
different languages, different religions
A plural society, unity in diversity
keeping off diversity
Safely she passed through
Religious tortures, political killings
Foiled all attempts at conversion
A haven for refugees,
Jews, Tibetans and Parsis.
Fight with non-violence
Shook the foundations of
The Mighty British Empire
It was really a wonder
She also fought violence
With violence
on occasions with greater thunder.
She has the nuclear capacity
Her peaceful nature avoids rapacity
Now inundating America
With Software
All other nations looking with stare
The biggest democracy of the world,
Soiled by corruption and crime,
Too much of democracy,
Courts Western, justice desi
Still my Bharat
did not lose her soul
Stands like rock with Noble high goal.

My Wife

My wife is a Godly gift
Full of affection, no rift
In action she is very swift
One night cold air coming
like a rill,
In half sleep she woke up,
Quickly the window was shut,
In the morning when window
was opened,
One lizard was found cut.
CAS is no problem for her.
She watches only two channels,
All other channels are our enemies
Corrupting our younger generation.
Like Buddhists she wants 'Nirwaan'
Kirtan, Pooja, Prayer are her '*Praan*.'
Like a traditional wife she
Does not call me by my name,
I am her J. Jee, hey Jee.
As a teacher she built up
with full zeal her nation

At full ration.
She is an eternal teacher,
She taught her own
children,
Now she teaches her grand-children.
She thinks Americans are prosperous
Because they don't care for dress
She uses limited clothes without press.
Campa Cola, Pepsi are an attack
on our civilisation and culture,
These should be treated like vultures.
Anything precious she keep in a place,
where it is difficult to trace.
She has produced three diamonds,
one has been taken by Americans,
other two have been left behind.
They are serving—the nation
With full attention.

New York

When I went to see New York
I did not find it new
this is my own view
It was dilapidated and old
Now neither silver nor gold.
The grand two towers
lost their bowers
From their rubbles smoke
was rising high towards the sky.
The commercial capital
of America was shaken
down, the trade
scattered all around.
I did not find it
different from the
Indian commercial capital
Bombay, small lanes—
crowded streets, small shops
But even then it gives hopes
It has trains running
underground, mother

earth is kind, destruction
it will wind,
Again to glory will bind
Its nights are days and days nights
It acted as a
wall against Washington
It bore the brunt of all attacks
It saved Pentagon and House White.

Oh God

Who you are?
what you are?
where you are?
since time immemorial
People have been
on the search
Declaring you a mystery

Some found you sitting
Shining on a throne
In the seventh Heaven
Some say God is all light
Dazzling, puzzling and muzzling

I don't find him confined
when I look at the Sea
Impressed am I by might
of the Powerful waves,
The inherent creative energy
The smiling flowers indicate
His colourfulness, strength and beauty

The beautiful vales
His grandeur they hail,
Oh God,! in the lightning
You appear like a flash,
The rivers reflect
His tenderness and flow of life
In the clouds we find
pleasantness and plenty

You are all love
In the form of a mother
All discipline in the
form of a soldier,
All innocence in
the form of a child
Your seat is in
the human heart
Full of compassion
And mercy.

Your angry aspects
Are the storms,
The Wars, the Famine,
Oh Lord! Do you
Punish those who defy you
who commit crimes against humanity
To bring them back to sanity?

The Politician

The politician a rendition
of sedition
That was born
Millions of years ago
In the shape of
Adam and Eve.

Promises are meant
To be broken
Didn't Adam launch
the tradition first?

Never says what he wills
Never wills what he says
Eggs others on
to march ahead.
Lets them march
Remains behind
When errors creep in
Rushes in to chide.

With flames in eyes

he asks them
What they did
And why?
That's not what he wanted
he wanted this
he wanted that
What actually he wanted
Let there be no chat.

Talk he must
on everything
under the sun
sense on nonsense
Nonsense on sense
Why, how and whence?

Life is like that
Comic in tragic
Tragic in comic
Adulteration works
Purity falls flat.

Sing of peace with
Sword in one hand
A pen in the other
which is mightier?
sword or the pen?
women or the men?
cock or the hen?

Be in no hurry
To decide
only enjoy the ride.

Lies have a right
To exist along with truth
No killings,
Ahimsa parmodharma.

The uncouth folks
May walk out or in
May yell or make a din
Never mind missiles
Of Eggs and tomatoes
Be they rotten
Be calm and cool
Like the fluffy wool
That makes no sound
When you beat

Eat back your words
Every word has a
Taste of its own
graces and disgrace
a part of
The game of life.
Play the game well
without any pell-mell.

The Primitive and The Modern Man

The primitive man looked
within to understand others
Mother, father and brothers.
The modern man critically
Analyses and weighs
Everything that comes his ways.
The primitive poured out
his heart when he spoke.
The modern uses wiles,
Hides back his real intentions.
Modern civilisation had
Its roots in the past,
Like a nursling it was
Reared by the nurse
of sincerity, devotion and clarity.
Modern civilisation is being
Fed by cunning and deception
What a progress have
We made,

There is no basis
Roof and shade,
The flowers grow
But colours fade.
The crops grow without any taste,
The clouds come without
Any rain,
The rivers flow without
Any glow.
We are sitting on volcanoes
of arms,
Wars fought without rules.
Swords and spears do not
Come in the open
Bravery is only a token
Battle is only a deception
Will we go to live on Mars or Moon?
How long, how soon?

Publisher

Publisher is a well-wisher
of the Author, the creator
Slowly creator becomes a waiter
At his well-wisher's table,
Waiting for the fallen crumbs.

The roles are reversed
Blessing turns into curse
Every Publisher wants hot shot
He is in search of a golden pot
He thinks of the golden hen
His eyes are on the dollar and yen.

Publisher is a skilful gambler
A businessman traveller
He knows how to win
God gifted him with trade acumen.

He reserves riches for self
For the Author name and fame

His selection is always the best
Without any test
He gets only wealth
Which fades before fame,
Wealth is lower than name
A balanced game.

Separation

Separation a spade
to dig up memories
from the ruins
of the past.

Cancer of monotony
born of meetings frequent
needs an operation.

A pain not in vain
forces inquest within
which opens up
the main spring of life.

Waste tears no more
let them grow into pearls
in the dark cells
of the turbulent heart
to be offered at
the feet of the Lord.

Teacher

A teacher must teach
how to read how to write
What is wrong what is right.

'A' for Apple, one two three
This is the job preliminary
This is to spread literacy
May be college or school
He must stand, no sitting on stool

With knowledge he must walk
His helpers are black-board
And chalk

In the end he is to preach
High goals, to ennoble the soul
He is to produce good citizen

He is to build a nation
He must be a model

Of virtues,
He must fight against
Superstitions.

If he forgets his role
Runs after wealth,
destroys nation's health
He fails as a Teacher
He turns out to be
A cheater.

Two Whistles

First Whistle
Blow thy whistle
Oh guard!
The sweet music
of thy whistle
will remove the thistle
of separation
from the Lord.

On the tiny waves
floats a melody
causing ripples of rapture
in the lake of heart

Guard attired in
spotlessly while
looks like an angle,
this whistle a call
to unite with the Lord.

Second Whistle

Time to depart
sorrowful heart
What a jarring note!
No more, whistle no more
Rustling of leaves
falling from the trees
sounds a note of warning

Guard attired in spotlessly while
looks like a ghost
causing tears, fears
wounds from the spears

Union

A surging crowd
of aspirations and hopes
Pressing at the portals
of the heart

Tongues in eyes
eyes in tongues
The preconceived harangue
melts into a stare
At a place where
Different colours share
A lissome beauty

Eyes into eyes
lips on lips
Fingers on hips
Heaving breasts
Warming the chest
Magic of love
At its best.

Two souls merge into one
Engaged in thoughtlessness
Lost in bliss
In the heart of hiss
Words melt into tears,
Flow out from
the innermost spheres
Drowning all plaints.

Feeling with hands
Thinking with heart
Silence looks trim & smart.

Washington

Washington all white
Full of light
Seat of American might
It decides, what is wrong
what is right.
Clean, pollution free
From communism it
made Russia free
It freed Afghanistan
of communism and communalism
It fights for Democracy
In America, as well as outside
It keeps its sphere wide
It wipes out dictatorship
with severe lashes and whips
President in White House
Acts as a cop of the world
He is super to UNO
He freed Iraq
with all His herd.
He has got godly powers

New York lost its towers
but Washington kept safe
Its bowers
He has won wars and battles
America does not care
for any ism
He is now after terrorism,
Terrorism is after him
Some countries are running
Terrorists camps
No success until are
closed these vamps.
He is waiting for
Proper time to strike
without any slogan or mike.

Why is it So?

When in Kerala
I used to think of Delhi
With its different seasons
Without any reasons.
New Delhi with all its greenery
And beautiful buildings
As scenery.

Its Red Fort takes us back
to the splendour and
grandeur of the Moghuls.
Her Qutab Minar tells
us of height of flight.
Whether wrong or right.
The meandering, sunny
And smiling Jamuna,
The cultural auditoria
India Gate without Victoria.
Well-guarded Presidential Palace.
My small cozy, lovely home,
My loving wife, my innocent

children.
Birla Mandir where the
Greatest soul rose to heaven
My good friends,
My good neighbours.
I longed to see them.
Daily I used to pray
To God to send me
Back to Delhi.

One day God in
His happy mood
granted my wish.
For a few days in Delhi
I forgot Kerala,
Lost in parties and dinners.
When all this was over
I felt sour,
Kerala licked back
My memory.
The God's own country,
Her beautiful sea
Waves bathing the shores,
Her lovely lagoons,
Attractive back waters and
Lush-green trees
Her graceful women

With blithe figures,
big dark eyes and long
lustrous hair,
Flashing the mind every where.

Kovalam Beach (a beauty to reach)
The glorious sun set
At Shanghmugham,
Sun as a pitcher of
Attractive fire, going down
In the sea to get cool
and calm
Again I long to go
Back to Kerala.
Why is it so
I don't know.

Working Wife

At a school in Delhi,
For a handful of silver,
My love, I mortgaged.
Always I worshipped Venus,
Never the god of Mammon,
What happened, am amazed.
There is nothing in me
Perhaps, to attract her,
Or where is she engaged?
Loathed are part-time wives,
Even that much is not she;
On me all eyebrows raised.
I dreamt of a home, little,
Sweet home, still a dream,
In my lonely fancy caged.
For her sake, against
Dear ones and Near ones,
Useless battles I waged.
In this age of cash,
In this age of commerce,
Alas, by helplesness chased.

Married, no doubt, am I,
But worse than bachelors,
Self-condemned, never praised.
Twice I went to her, twice,
Not once she came to me,
What a wife? Godly graced.
Around Fire we took a vow
Together to live and die,
Is the Fire into ashes changed?
Quite near Gandhi's Samadhi
Lives my love, unmindful
Of the role Kasturba played.